CHICKS & DUCKS
. . . AS PETS

JACK C. HARRIS

Contents

NTRODUCTION, ...**4**
Varieties of chickens, 6; Different kinds of ducks, 13; Transporting your new pet, 17

HOUSING, ...**20**
A house for chicks, 20; Housing and ponds for ducklings, 29

FEEDING, ...**34**
Chicks and chickens, 34; Ducklings and ducks, 38

HEALTH, ...**42**
Your chicken's health, 42; Your duck's health, 47

YOUR PET, ...**52**
Chicks as pets, 52; Ducks as pets, 58

INDEX, ...**64**

PHOTO CREDITS

Many thanks are due to the wonderful photographers who share the love of poultry with me. I hope the list below is complete. If I have forgotten anyone, please forgive me. The listing is by the date on which I received them.

Isabelle Francais, Michael Gilroy, Robert Pearcy, Horst Mueller, Dr. Herbert R. Axelrod, Gary Hersch, Michael Baumeister, P. Leysen, Heinz Meyer, Helmut Neubueser and Hans Reinhard.

Distributed in the UNITED STATES by T.F.H. Publications, Inc., One T.F.H. Plaza, Neptune City, NJ 07753; in CANADA to the Pet Trade by H & L Pet Supplies Inc., 27 Kingston Crescent, Kitchener, Ontario N2B 2T6; Rolf C. Hagen Ltd., 3225 Sartelon Street, Montreal 382 Quebec; in CANADA to the Book Trade by Macmillan of Canada (A Division of Canada Publishing Corporation), 164 Commander Boulevard, Agincourt, Ontario M1S 3C7; in ENGLAND by T.F.H. Publications, PO Box 15, Waterlooville PO7 6BQ; in AUSTRALIA AND THE SOUTH PACIFIC by T.F.H. (Australia) Pty. Ltd., Box 149, Brookvale 2100 N.S.W., Australia; in NEW ZEALAND by Ross Haines & Son, Ltd., 82 D Elizabeth Knox Place, Panmure, Auckland, New Zealand; in the PHILIPPINES by Bio-Research, 5 Lippay Street, San Lorenzo Village, Makati, Rizal; in SOUTH AFRICA by Multipet Pty. Ltd., P.O. Box 35347, Northway, 4065, South Africa. Published by T.F.H. Publications, Inc. Manufactured in the United States of America by T.F.H. Publications, Inc.

There are dozens of different races and breeds of chickens, and many color varieties within each race and breed. This young girl is holding a German breed called the *Watermaalsche Bartzwerge*. The bird is a hen and is a dwarf variety which is now becoming popular worldwide.

Every year as spring arrives and the Easter season is upon us, there are a number of pet stores offering newborn chicks and baby ducklings as pets for children. There is nothing greater than the delighted expression of a child who finds one of these cheeping (or quacking) balls of fluff in his/her basket on Easter morning. Unfortunately, there is nothing worse than the disheartened cries of the same child a few months later when the chick or duckling has either died or has to be given away because it has outgrown its shoe box or similar makeshift home.

INTRODUCTION

The main reason these tragedies occur is that the parents lack planning or understanding regarding the simple needs of these little birds. More and more humane societies urge parents not to give the gift of an animal on holidays because they fear that the recipient of the animal has not received the proper instruction concerning the care of the new charge.

Our aim is not to offer a scientific dissertation on barnyard fowl. What we are presenting in these pages is straight-forward information and a simple set of guidelines for those who are either planning on giving a chick or duckling as a present, or have received such a gift and have no idea of how to care for the animal. Too often, people treat farm and wild animals in their care the same way they treat domesticated house pets such as dogs and cats: feeding them when they want to be fed, bathing them when the keeper feels they need it, and playing with them whenever convenient. Often these people either totally ignore or are completely unaware of the specific and different needs animals such as chicks and ducklings require for survival.

After reading the information here, pet owners will have a working knowledge as to how to care for, feed, and protect their birds from common dangers and diseases. Those deciding on whether or not to give these creatures as gifts will be able to make an educated decision based on whether their recipient will be able to provide for the new pet's needs.

As always, if any questions or problems arise regarding chicks and ducklings (or any pet for that matter) that are not covered in this volume, the pet owners are urged to seek the advice of their local pet shop proprietors. They are your local experts and your source of any informa-

Which came first, the chicken or the egg? The answer is both or either. The chicken evolved from fish-like ancestors which lived in the sea. The feathers are closely related to a fish's scales or animals' hair. Think about this: The unborn chick swims within the egg and breathes almost like a fish!

tion regarding your pet's requirements.

Although they're both common barnyard birds and can get along well together, chickens and ducks are very different and they require different kinds of care. There are some similarities, but basically they're separate species. For this reason, this book alternates between chicken and duck information. Some facts may be repeated, but for the most part the things you need to know for each kind of pet are contained in their own individual chapters. Also included is some background and historical information regarding the different breeds of chickens and ducks. Any pet is more enjoyable if you know something about its background and origin. Further information can be obtained from your pet shop dealer or local school library.

With a little planning, a pet duckling or chick will not only survive, but will provide years of pleasure and learning for a youngster. That goal is the reason for this book.

VARIETIES OF CHICKENS

The familiar chicken is of the species *Gallus gallus* or *G. domesticus*. Female chickens less than a year old are called pullets. Females older than this are referred to as hens. The males are called cocks or roosters. Very young chickens of either sex are all called chicks.

Although it is a bird, *Gallus gallus* has adapted to existence on the ground like the quail, pheasant, and turkey (the other commonly recognized members of *G. domesticus*). Being ground creatures, their natural diets consist of seeds, worms, insects, greens, etc. The chicken is recognized by its large body and short wings, which are not designed for actual

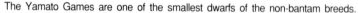

The Yamato Games are one of the smallest dwarfs of the non-bantam breeds.

This fine Italian Rooster is characterized by its single comb and white ear-lobes.

flying over anything but very short stretches. The enlarged area of the throat or gullet of the chicken (called the "crop") is large and the gizzard (a bird's "second stomach" used for grinding food) is strongly muscular.

Although more prominent on the male, all chickens have a naked, fleshy crest called a comb which decorates the head. Depending on the breed of chicken, the comb, is of different shapes and sizes. One variation is the Malay fowl's strawberry comb, which is set near the bird's eyes and is small and rounded. The La Fleche fowl's comb resembles a diminutive pair of horns. The Brahma is recognized by its pea comb, which has three serrated edges. The two-ridged leaf comb is characteristic of the French Houdan. There are endless variations of these and other combs due to cross-breeding and hereditary and dietary factors.

The same is true for the size and plumage of chickens. A full-grown chicken can weigh 12 pounds or more, as do some Brahma cocks. Others may weigh as little as 20 ounces, as is the case of the Bantam. Feather colors range from white, gray, yellow, blue, red, brown, and black.

Originally, the domesticated chicken came from southwestern Asia. Charles Darwin classified it as being descendant from a single species of jungle fowl (Red Jungle Fowl) still found wild in India today. More modern zoologists attribute its development as coming from a number of similar birds, all subdivisions of *Gallus gallus*.

Ancient Chinese documents make mention of the chicken, placing its introduction in that part of the world at about 1400 BC. This makes the chicken one of the very first domesticated animals mentioned in modern recorded history. Wild chickens date back even further in history, however, being found in Babylonian carvings and in early Greek texts. The Romans considered cocks as symbols of courage and believed all chickens to be sacred to Mars, their god of war.

There are many varieties of chicks that are suitable as pets for children. Your pet shop owner will be able to direct you to the kinds he has in stock–but it's always best to go prepared with a little background knowledge of your own before making a final selection. To the passerby, one chicken might seem the same as any other, especially in the younger stage where they all appear to be little yellow peeping balls of fluff. There are, in fact, a great number of varieties of chickens, each with its own particular plumage and often with its own particular disposition.

In the United States, American Plymouth Rocks, Mediterranean Leghorns, New Hampshires and the Rhode Island Reds are the most common kinds given as Easter gifts mainly because of their generally quiet natures. The Rhode Island Reds are distinguished from the New Hampshires by their deeper red plumage, black tails, and the occasional appearance of black wing feathers. The only preliminary drawback for any of these American varieties is that they grow quite large. The exception

This is a striped Wyandotte Bantam rooster.

is the Leghorns which remain small, but mature more quickly than the other kinds. Some experts consider them the most attractive variety of American chicken, an aspect which might become important to someone selecting one for a pet. All of these breeds of chicken are quick to feather and are known for laying eggs very well.

9

The Araucana is a Brazilian Indian name for this early descendent of a chicken. It has no tail and its legs are restrained so the bird won't run off.

The Brahma, Cochin, and Lanshan are all Asiatic chickens known for having quiet and gentle temperaments, making them good candidates for pets. If the pet owner doesn't want a collection of eggs to dispense with, one of the Asiatic varieties might be a better choice since they are not known for laying eggs as well as their American counterparts.

INTRODUCTION

Exotic Bantam and other mixed-breed chickens exist in great numbers; and they are often bred for the beauty of their features. While some are imported to the United States, the majority are bred in the U.S. They are enthusiastically exhibited at shows and local county fairs across the country. Anyone interested in raising and caring for such exotic chickens should learn as much as they can about the selective breeding process. They must learn which birds have desired characteristics, as even one chicken who is sub-standard can weaken the entire flock. Since the genetic traits of the Red Jungle Fowl (the recognized common ancestor of even the fanciest of chickens) are dominant, any exotic chickens penned

There are many kinds of chicken breeds. It is even possible for you to develop your own breed of chickens. Take a rooster and hen which you like (preferably from two different breeds) and breed them. Then select the chicks which look the best for the particular qualities you admire, and breed them back to the parent. You keep doing this until all of the offspring look like the birds you have envisioned. It sounds easy but can take many years depending upon the qualities for which you are breeding.

together for a few generations will produce nothing but Red Jungle Fowls.

Keeping specific breeds with individuals having desired genetic traits is actually the only special treatment keepers of exotic chickens have to worry about. The regular habits of these birds are similar to those of common chickens in every other respect.

DIFFERENT KINDS OF DUCKS

Although commonly called ducks, only about half of those waddling water birds with the flat bills are ducks. In fact, a "duck" is the female while the males are called "drakes." The males can be more easily distinguished because, as is the case with most birds, they are more brightly colored than the females. This is so that the male can attract more attention in the wild, thus leaving the female protected.

This is a German breed called the Krüper. It has white eggs and reaches a maximum weight of 5 pounds. It also comes in white. It is a nice dwarf species which is elongated and close to the ground.

This is the Pekin duck which originated in China. Pekin ducks are readily tamable, and that's why they are so popular as pets. They cross with wild Mallard ducks and many ponds are evidence of the flightless crosses between these two ducks. See the illustration on page 15.

Ducks are very similar to swans and geese but have shorter legs and shorter necks. They are further distinguished by the back scales on their legs. Swans and geese have front leg scales. The duck's land waddle is caused by its legs being positioned far back on its body. This makes walking difficult but allows for more powerful swimming. Their feathers are very soft and dense, making them virtually waterproof.

Scientifically, there are three classifications of duck subfamilies: the Anatidae, or freshwater ducks; the Merginae, or mergansers; and the Fuligulinae, or sea ducks. The most common duck is the all-white, yellow skinned Pekin duck, which originated in China. It was introduced in the United States in the early 1870s. A healthy Pekin is distinguished by its deep orange bill and feet. Full grown, the drake Pekin weighs about nine pounds, while the hen weighs around eight pounds. The drake's quack is also higher pitched than the hen's and his tail features have a characteristic curl. Docile, the Pekins are also extremely easy to tame as a children's pet—another reason for their overwhelming popularity in the United States.

In England, the Aylesbury duck is more popular. Its plumage is a brighter white than that of the Pekins and it has more weight in its breast. This variety of duck was also popular in the U.S. prior to the introduction of the Pekin, but it was discovered that the Pekin was generally heartier than the Aylesbury.

Originating in South America, the Muscovy duck is found in both white and dark varieties. Unlike the Aylesbury and the Pekin, the Muscovy duck is not believed to be descended from the wild Mallard. They are very quiet ducks and have often been called the "quackless ducks," even though they do make sounds.

The Buff is a variety of the Orpington breeds and there are four additional varieties known to exist. The American Buff has a rich, fawn buff color while the English Buff is more reddish. The Black is distinguished by its white bib and the Blue Buff has a slate bluish bib and two white primaries on each wing. Buffs have blue pupils unless they have been the result of some kind of crossbreeding. They are slightly smaller than the Aylesburys and the Pekins.

The Cayuga is a strain of duck produced from those found near Cayuga Lake in New York State. It's believed to be the result of a crossbreeding with an East Indian duck producing black plumage. These heavy birds are often raised for exhibition in shows around the world.

The Rouen has coloring very similar to a wild Mallard, but it weighs too much to fly. It was developed in England and is imported to the U.S.

Crossbreeding of chickens and ducks probably has been practiced since before recorded history, being done for the meat, the plumage, for size, or for other reasons. Because of this, there are a number of birds that appear to have characteristics of two or more of the specified breeds. Since most pet chicks and ducklings are bought when they are only chicks, it's usually impossible for the novice to know what the bird will look like when it is mature. This is why you should always select your pet bird from an experienced pet store owner who will be able to tell you what kind of chick or duckling you have selected and will be able to inform you of their mature appearance and size as well as their housing and feeding requirements.

In the United States, try and find a pet shop that indicates that their chicks are U.S. Pollorum Clean. This will certify that the chicks have been inspected and are free of any diseases.

As Pekins grow up, the family refuses to eat it, so they liberate the duck into the nearest large pond. In most cases this is a slow death for the bird...a butcher's knife would have been more thoughtful. This bird is a cross between a Pekin and a wild Mallard. Many of these crossings are flightless birds, like this one. Almost all domesticated ducks derived from the Mallard.

Raising and training a more exotic variety of duck is a separate and distinct hobby all its own. Many owners of home ponds or private aviaries keep such ducks simply for the decorative beauty of their plumage. The fact that even exotic ducks get along well with other birds such as peacocks, doves, and pigeons contributes to their appeal.

If interested, potential exotic duck owners can contact their local pet shop to inquire as to the location of local duck breeders. The prices of such birds will likely be more expensive than the common pet ducks due to their rarity and the expense of selective breeding.

If you select such a bird and it has to be imported, expect a delay. Many countries require by law any bird entering from a foreign country

There are many breeds of duck. Not only are there differences in size but also in color. Not many ducks are flightless, so you have to be careful about the ducks you select for your pond. Larger ducks bully the smaller breeds when it comes to fighting for the feed.

to be quarantined for at least two weeks at a quarantine center. Poultry and game bird regulations have been set up for the protection of all birds and their owners. Luckily, since this practice has been widespread there are many exotic birds being bred around the world, making the quarantine unnecessary and the expense less.

Wild game ducks and exotic ducks should be completely penned in an aviary which includes a clean pond and nests provided under trees and shrubs. Their habits are similar to the more common breeds of duck, so no out-of-the-ordinary arrangements have to be made for their care. There are national and international duck shows for exhibiting such birds.

Your local pet shop, bird breeder, veterinarian, or library can provide information regarding these shows.

TRANSPORTING YOUR NEW PET

Most good pet stores will provide you with the proper carrying case or box in which to take your pet bird home safely. However, here are some guidelines set down by fowl experts regarding the transportation of ducks and chickens. These authorities are usually concerned about transporting the birds from farms to stockyards, but their methods can be easily adapted by the pet owner since their goals are the same: safe transport of the birds from one place to another.

When transporting birds in any moving vehicle, it's certain that some of them will be jostled around a bit while trying to maintain their balance if they are allowed to stand. Birds are in quite a bit of danger during these trips, for wings could be broken, legs sprained, feathers damaged, etc. If a bird suffers a cut, the bleed-

If you want to buy your child a duckling for Easter (a tradition), or just so she can have an inexpensive, hardy pet (they can be kept outdoors all year), be sure you learn how to care for them. The duck grows up...keep that in mind!

A pair of wild Mallard ducks. Mallards are found worldwide in the climates where there is nearby ice during the winter. They are very friendly and stay close to civilization. They cross with most pet ducks because most pet ducks were derived from Mallard strains... The male is the more colorful of the pair.

ing could cause the other birds to pull and peck at the wound, making it infected-or worse.

The best way to avoid such problems is to transport the birds in a container that will not allow them to stand. Special crates are made for chickens and ducks that are designed to be safely stacked tightly together while still allowing for plenty of air. Naturally, a pet owner is not going to want a full-size chicken or duck crate to take a single bird home in, but a look at the design of these boxes will give one a good idea as to what is required for safe travel.

If you can't obtain a small enough crate or box, you can get a larger one and fill the bottom with straw to lessen the height. If you are transporting more than one bird, you can pack them together side by side so that there will be less space for them to bounce around in.

You have to consider air for the birds. Too little ventilation will cause the birds to become overheated; too much air will chill them and increase the danger of respiratory infection. No matter what kind of container you finally use, be certain that the air can enter and leave freely.

A good way to check the temperature of your transport box is to place the bird inside and close it up. Wait a few minutes and then slide your hand into the closed box so you can feel the air surrounding your pet. It should not feel uncomfortably warm. If it is too hot, you will probably notice too much dampness caused by the bird's own respiration. To be extra sure that the temperature is proper, use a thermometer in the closed box. Leave it there for two minutes and then read it. The birds will be comfortable at a reading of 65°F (18°C); but, if it's a hot day, this temperature may be too extreme. You might have to cut more holes in the box or crate to allow for additional ventilation. Never allow the temperature to rise above 80°F (26°C) in the transport box.

Chickens do not have sweat glands. They expel excess heat through their respiratory system, making them pant when overheated, much as a dog might do. If you see your birds panting, it's another sign that extra ventilation is required. Don't ever cut the holes larger than the bird's head. This will allow the air to enter and escape, but it will keep the bird from getting loose.

When you load the box, make sure that the holes are not up against anything that will block the air flow. If you're riding in a closed vehicle, be sure to have the air conditioning on or one of the windows opened.

One of the worst things some people have done in the past is to transport chickens in the closed trunk of their car. For some reason they are surprised when they open up the trunk and find the birds sprawled out, having trouble moving and breathing, or already dead.

If your birds are transported in comfort, they can survive for many hours without food or water. These birds like routine and sameness in their lives. Once they have settled down in their own home areas, try to avoid moving them in vehicles unless absolutely necessary.

Most pet ducks can live on grass alone, but they should be fed a specially prepared duck food so they will have a balanced diet. These Diepholz geese were bred for grazing. Geese and ducks both belong to the family *Anatidae*.

S ince the keeping of ducks and chicks as pets has grown in popularity over the years, there are a number of commercial pet houses on the market for both chicks and ducklings. Talk over the possibility of purchasing one of these from your local pet supplier. They will be able to recommend the proper commercial house you need or give you valuable tips on how you can

HOUSING

build the proper shelter for your new pets. In any case, be certain you have the proper housing prepared before you purchase your pet chick or duckling.

A HOUSE FOR CHICKS

The very first thing that must be done prior to making the decision to buy a pet chick or duckling is to make certain you have the space and facilities to house one properly. Unlike cats and dogs, chicks and ducklings cannot be allowed the free run of your house. If you already have a cat or dog in your home then it is imperative that you make plans to protect your new bird pet from these animals. Even if your cat or dog is only curious about the new pet, the methods of satisfying that curiosity could be fatal to a new born chick or duckling.

If you are getting a newly born chick, then before you select one you should investigate the possibility of buying a brooder. The initial four weeks of a baby chick's life are crucial. If the chick survives that long, there is a good chance that it received a good start in life and will have a better chance to persevere. Since warmth is of primary importance to a young chick's survival, a brooder of some kind is necessary. Even a slight drop in temperature can spell disaster for these fragile young animals.

A brooder is relatively inexpensive. Its construction is simple, being comprised of a covering and a light bulb. It should be designed so that it can adequately protect chicks from predators such as rats and snakes as well as drafts and dampness. Some people who have large areas of property or who live on farms have climate-controlled chicken houses which work like giant brooders. City or suburban dwellers have reported success by setting up small brooders in their garages or basements. As long as these areas are dry, then they should be sufficient.

While it is important to keep the brooder safe from drafts, chick owners must remember that they must not eliminate ventilation. If the temperature rises, windows should be opened to increase circulation.

Baby chicks can spend the first few months in your house, restrained in a cardboard box. Then they grow up. You have to be prepared for this situation. Chickens make fine pets until they start crowing at dawn!

Holding a sheet of tissue paper around the brooder is an excellent way to check for drafts. If the tissue remains vertical and hangs still, then the area is probably safe.

While the majority of people buying pet chicks buy only one at a time, two or more chicks may be purchased simultaneously. It's perfectly all right for more than one chick to share a brooder as long as adequate space is provided. A wooden box about two feet square would make an excellent brooder for multiple chicks. However, if you observe

Incubators are available from most pet shops or feed stores. They keep the inside of the box about 95°F. They can be used to hatch eggs or to keep the chicks warm before they are feathered.

one chick pecking or bothering another, install a red-colored light bulb. A tin can nailed to the top with a 60 to 100 watt light bulb suspended from it will provide the needed warmth. Some chick owners have reported success with brooders constructed out of an 18-inch wide roll of corrugated cardboard held together with clothespins. An electric or infrared lamp is suspended above it. This brooder can be easily expanded as the chick(s) grow larger. As soon as you are able to determine the sex of your chicks, separate the hens from the roosters.

The heat in these brooders should read about 95°F (35°C) measured from the outside edge at approximately two inches from the floor. The humidity should be kept between the 60% and 70% range. Dimmer light bulbs are recommended. If it is too bright, the chicks will not eat during the night. Don't make the brooder so small that it's impossible for the chicks to move away from the heat. They have to be able to move away from the heat when necessary. You should also make provisions in case power is lost. A wood-burning stove or a gas heater can provide emergency heat as long as the area remains well ventilated.

You should spread a two-inch deep layer of litter on the brooder floor. One expert recommends a mixture of three parts shavings and one part peat moss as ideal. Other materials, such as finely chopped hay, granulated corncobs, peat moss by itself, sawdust, shredded sugar cane, or straw, have also been used successfully. No matter what material you use, the litter should be stirred frequently and completely changed every three days or so. Some chicks may try to eat various mixtures. Since some of this material could prove dangerous or even fatal, it's best to cover the litter with burlap for a couple of days. Never cover a brooder floor with newspapers. A chick's feet cannot maintain any traction on such a surface and its legs will spread apart.

After approximately two weeks, the brooder temperature should be reduced about five degrees. Every week thereafter, the heat should be reduced an additional five degrees until the supplemental heat is no longer required for the chicks' health. When the chicks have grown healthy feathers and appear ready to roost, the temperature can be lowered to within the 65 to 70°F (18—20°C) range. Chicks usually require auxiliary heat for about 12 weeks if they were born in the winter or early spring. Late spring and early summer chicks can usually forego extra heat after only six weeks.

Since chicks grow quickly into chickens, brooders are only temporary shelters. Before deciding to raise a chick, permanent quarters must be prepared. In some cases, brooders may be designed in such a way that small roosts can be included when needed. Young chickens enjoy roosting, but this desire often depends on the breed. For instance, Leghorns may be seen roosting at four weeks of age while some of the larger breeds will not begin roosting until they are from six to seven weeks old.

If it is closed in and protected from rodents, cool breezes, and severe weather, the developing or growing pen may be used as a poultry shelter as the young chick or chickens mature. An existing structure such as a tool or bicycle shed, a safe area of a garage, a stall in a barn, or a playhouse can be transformed into a sheltering area for young chickens. The one general requirement is that there must be at least two square feet of floor space for each bird. If a shelter is any smaller than this, or if it has a low ceiling, it should be made portable so it can be easily moved in case of temperature extreme. Screened window openings are also necessary. There should be at least one square foot of such openings for each ten square feet of floor space.

Any chicken housing structure must be kept clean. Hot soapy water should be used to brush down cobwebs and dirt from the shelter's ceiling and walls. If you paint and disinfect the shelter, do so at least a month before you plan to house any chickens, since the fumes of certain paints and cleaning chemicals may produce poisonous or dangerous fumes.

Nothing elaborate is needed to install the required roosting perches. Common dowel sticks set back against the far wall of the shelter will be adequate as long as they are protected against any drafts. The first perches built should be close to the floor of the shelter, with others stepped up higher. A flat, smooth board can be used under perches to catch any droppings. This board should be installed so it can be removed for easy cleaning. The area under the perches should be screened off so smaller young chickens can't get into the waste material. The same litter material you used for the brooder can be used here. As with the brooder, you should stir the litter often and make certain it is clean and dry. Chickens have a tendency to scratch litter from windows and openings toward the rear of their shelter. Any litter that has so accumulated should be sifted toward the front of the shelter every day with a rake or pitch fork.

Chickens will enjoy lying in the little gullies they create in the litter. They'll stretch one of their legs out and, flapping their wings wildly, throw the litter all over their bodies. If you see this happening, don't worry; it's very natural and even beneficial to them. The particles of litter filter down through their feathers and settle on their skin. This action can actually smother lice, which can then be shaken loose. However, this dust bathing should not be relied on as a cure-all for lice.

You may see the same sort of action by baby chicks in their feed. The action is instinctive and it does not necessarily mean that they are suffering from lice infestation. The vigorous dusting is to the chickens as a scratch behind the ear is to a dog or cat–its soothing and they simply enjoy it.

If your litter mixture is made up of particles too large to serve as a dust bath, your pet may enjoy a separate dust bath container. Place a container filled with about six inches of loose sand in the chicken's house. The container should be about two feet tall and two feet square. On occasion, sprinkle wood ashes or lice powder in with the sand. Don't place the box under the roost or else the sand will become contaminated and dangerous for the chickens to use. Keep the box in direct sunlight as often as possible so the chickens won't be tempted to use it as a nesting place.

Remember, all food and water for chickens must always be in a shaded area so that the food will not be contaminated by sun exposure. Additionally, all hoppers for food should be larger than those for baby chicks. To make certain the food isn't spoiled by the chickens' scratching habits, the hoppers should be slightly elevated. The same is true for water containers. You must be certain that all water is protected from chicks getting into it. Unless an area is screened off, it's a good practice to place a wire mesh platform on the floor directly beneath the water hopper.

A yard, screened on all sides and the top, should be installed, since young chickens enjoy their exercise. Such a yard does not have to be large, but it must be designed so there are no sharp corners anywhere. Young chickens might crowd into corners if they are fearful or uncertain about new surroundings. If your developing quarters for young chickens

Many chickens cannot fly, though their original ancestors could. The same is true of turkeys. The wild ones fly while the domesticated ones refuse to fly.

This is a fighting cock youngster that can run fairly well. It took these two girls a few minutes to tire the bird out enough to catch him.

are not found to be adequate for mature chickens, a whole new shelter should be provided. If you have only one or a small flock of pet chicks, a simple house can be assembled on wheels, enabling it to be moved out of the hot sun or into shelter in wet weather. A mobile shelter like this can be a small wooden frame construction with a tar-paper peaked roof. The floor can be made of wire so droppings can fall to the ground or onto a removable tray positioned underneath. For the birds' comfort, the house should be large and roomy enough for a roost to be built above the wire floor. A 14-by-16 inch nest allows approximately enough space for four hens.

Additional materials would consist of a food hopper and a water pail. If these things are in a shady yard, where the chickens have easy access, then there is no need to crowd the chicken house with them. A screened patio box can be secured against the door of such a house.

A simple, open-sided, makeshift lean-to with a peaked roof

protecting the roosts is the most basic and common design for the average poultry house used for a few young chickens. It is only a couple of feet high from the roof to the ground. In the event of severe weather before the birds are strengthened by age and good diet, the sides of the lean-to can be safeguarded by closing them in with burlap or other similar and appropriate windbreaks. Chickens need more shielding against the elements in colder climates. The poultry house should be situated so its entrance faces either south or southeast. Even in warm climates, the house should be opened on the south or southeast. This will allow the chickens to receive maximum warmth during spring and winter months.

In more elaborately constructed shelters, vent holes at the roof line and even sliding glass windows are possible. The best kind of flooring for a permanent chicken house is concrete; but it should, of course, be covered by the same litter mixture you used in brooders and developing pens. The litter should be deep enough so the chickens can burrow in it during the warmer summer months. They like to do this since it helps them to remain cool. As was true in the earlier shelters, chickens like to scratch through their litter, moving it into heaps away from the windows or other openings. Litter accumulates at the rear of shelter and should be raked toward the front every day.

These Leghorns are bred for egg production. Most eggs eaten in America are Leghorn. Leghorn is the name of a town in Italy but this breed probably originated in America around 1850.

Roosts in the chicken house should measure from one to two-and-a-half feet above the floor and be evenly spaced from 13 to 15 inches apart. They should be located near the rear of the shelter and away from openings. They can be constructed from two-by-four or two-by-two boards if the corners are sanded so they are slightly rounded. Sharp edges of any kind should be avoided. Leghorns need about eight inches of perch space for each bird. Plymouth Rocks and other larger breeds require at least a ten-inch perch space per bird.

It is very important to keep your chicken house as clean as possible for the general well-being of your chickens. Droppings should be removed daily. There are several ways to make this task an easy one. Removable boards fitted beneath roosts can catch droppings effortlessly. They should be placed six or eight inches beneath the roosts so the birds cannot get to them. A board 20 inches wide should be adequate for one roost. Two roosts will probably require a 34-inch wide board. For safety, the boards should be sanded as smooth as possible. Select boards which are fairly free from cracks. A pit for droppings can be dug beneath the roosts too, but most experts suggest that the boards are more sufficient for just a few chickens since they are removable for easy cleaning.

Remember to equip your chicken house with good-sized food hoppers and place them at least a few inches above the shelter floor. You don't want the chickens' constant scratching to contaminate the food with litter or droppings. Earthen crocks or large galvanized iron water pails or pans are excellent as water containers. Their natural weight and size will prevent them from being too easily knocked over by the chickens' movements. Since they must also be protected from contamination, you should locate them on mesh wire mats approximately 18 inches above the floor. Another alternative is to secure food and water containers to the roosts.

Nests for your chicken house should measure about 14-by-16 inches and should be fixed on the end of the shelter walls or on any partitions you may have installed. Secure them high enough so the chickens can move about easily beneath them. To allow for ventilation, the back and ends of nests can be formed out of wire. Low-cost nests can be simply built from old-fashioned orange boxes or egg crates. The nests should always be partially filled with clean straw, shavings, or sugar cane.

The best location for your chicken house (keeping in mind the proper south-faced entrance), is on a gently rolling slope. This allows for both good air circulation and proper drainage. The yard surrounding your chicken house should also provide for a safe environment for your pet chickens. If you let your chickens run in the yard, you may have to clip one wing, especially of lightweight breeds, so they can't fly. The yard should be as dry as possible and clear of any mud holes.

Ducks are not happy unless they have a pond in which to swim. Is there a more beautiful sight than a family of ducks with the mother teaching the children how to swim?

HOUSING AND PONDS FOR DUCKLINGS

Most barnyard fowl experts agree that ducks are far less trouble to raise than chickens. Newborn ducklings, if they have been separated from their mothers, need only be kept in a straw or shavings-lined box with a heating pad or light bulb for warmth until they are about ten days old. The straw or shavings should be changed every day. As they get older, however, they require not only some of the same housing considerations as chickens, but something more. The biggest housing difference between a pet duck as opposed to a pet chicken is the necessity of installing or having access to a duck pond. The potential duck owner who owns a large yard, a big field, or an orchard can probably build an adequate shelter to protect his young ducklings from predators such as hawks, rats, and other animals. Like chickens, ducks like a clean, dry house for sleeping. The shelter need not be complicated or elaborate. An inexpensive shelter against harsh weather can be easily made from as little as two pieces of square lumber by slanting them and making a tent-shaped house. Such a structure should be between four and five feet high. It should have a hinged opening so cleaning is easy. Dry straw makes a good nest, as long

29

as it is changed when it becomes soiled. It only takes a little weather-proofing on the sides to make certain the ducks will remain warm and dry.

If you're taking care of a whole flock of ducks, you should build what is commonly called a sleeping house. An ideal sleeping house for ducks should be about six feet square at the base, stand approximately five feet high in front, and measure four-and-a-half feet high at back. Don't be fooled by the old wives' tale about ducks not minding the rain. They like to be dry when they're sleeping. Be sure to install some kind of waterproofing on the roof. Construct a pair of center doors that open outward to make the daily cleaning job easier. Each duck house should be floored with one inch tarred boards. Standing the house on bricks will keep it much drier and make it much more durable to weather; however, these bricks should be stacked at least a foot apart to allow for good ventilation. Additonally, bricks stacked too close together outside make perfect nesting places for rats–known duck predators.

As was true in the case of chickens, ducks can make comfortable homes and nests in existing structures and spaces such as those found in tool sheds, empty barn stalls, or a corner of a garage or dry basement. In all cases, the floor should be kept covered with clean straw or shavings that can be changed every day.

Many homes have enough space to build a little duck pond in the yard, for nothing huge or elaborate is necessary. A very good duck pond can be easily made with as few materials as ready-mix cement and a drain pipe. It doesn't have to be any bigger than three feet by four feet, if your yard space is limited. The pond must not be too deep. Baby ducklings, although natural swimmers, can easily become water-logged and drown. Construct a gradual incline from the edge of the pond so the ducks won't slip when they exit or enter. Wooden cleats can be embedded in the cement before it hardens to make footing easier for the ducks. Building a pond near a sloping bank makes daily draining of the water easier. The pond must be cleaned every day since ducks do not like dirty water. They like clean water to swim in and for washing food particles off of themselves. Ducks prefer to mate while swimming–and this is another excellent reason for always providing water.

Some potential pet owners choose pet ducks because they already have a stream on their land. Even if such a stream is too wide to fence across, part of a duck pond can easily be fenced in near the stream bank. If this is done, the wire mesh fencing must be staked to the bottom of the stream. Not only can ducks swim, but they can dive too. Staking the fence at the bottom of the stream will prevent the ducks from diving under the fenced-in area. If you have different flocks of ducks, or if you're raising both chickens and ducks, these various bird flocks can be sepa-rated by running the chicken-wire right through the stream, as well as the

Different color ducklings mean different color adults. When buying pet ducks, be sure they are of the flightless variety, unless you want them to fly away when your child has lost interest in them.

adjoining fields. Ducks have no difficulty getting along with the chickens. They can also be fenced in with other birds and fowl such as peacocks, pigeons, and geese with no problems.

One duck expert describes a popular duck house design which is easily mobile. It is constructed on a wheelbarrow type base so that it can be hoisted and rolled to various locations around the yard. One immediate advantage of such an arrangement is that the lawn under the house won't die since the house is always in a different spot. It's also excellent for the ducks since they can be quickly moved out in the sunshine during the winter season and under the shade in the summer months. The wooden frame of the wheelbarrow measures about eight feet long and three feet wide and rests on one redwood wheel. Like a conventional wheelbarrow, the portable duck house has two handles for easy moving.

Secured to the top of this frame is a three-and-a-half foot high waterproof duck house with a slanting roof, a patio, and a shallow water tank. The house has about a two-and-a-half by three foot opening which leads out to the chicken wire patio. There is a wire floor in the duck house and over the patio area which allows the duck droppings to easily drop through to keep the birds clean. A removable tray under the wire floor in the duck house makes daily cleaning easy. This tray also keeps the house warmer than a wire bottom. The patio area has a removable tray which acts as a feed pad. It is removable for easy cleaning too, which should be done every day. The tray catches the old food, which drops through the open wire, thus preventing the ducks from eating contaminated food which could possibly make them sick.

A waterproofed plywood tank with all the points tarred can be situated on the wheelbarrow frame alongside the small patio. This tank should be designed to slope gradually and be fitted with wooden cleats on the sides to prevent the ducks from injuring themselves. If proper drains are installed at the bottom of the tank, it will be easier to keep the water clean. Only small amounts of water should be used for ducklings. Incubator ducklings have not developed the thick down feathers that keep them waterproof. The only protection they have is the weatherproofing the mother duck provides with her own glandular oil when she hatches them. These babies can easily drown in deep water.

You may have seen adult ducks swimming happily in holes in frozen ponds. They are able to withstand swimming in such icy water because of the thick coat of down under their outer waterproof plumage. Their thick web feet do not feel the cold temperatures at all. It is more important to protect ducks from the heat than from the cold. The entire wheelbarrow duck house and pond is overlaid with chicken wire for the general protection of the ducks as well as for good ventilation. It also allows plenty of sunshine. On days of extremely high temperatures, a lightweight covering can be secured over the top of the portable pen, if the yard has no suitable shade trees. Baby ducklings can be housed in portable duck house and pond combinations such as these except when they are grazing in the grass. At such times, someone should be keeping a close watch on them.

This is a lovely sight, a young girl restraining her new pet ducklings. However, they are exposed to the sun, cold wind and wild animals if kept in this cage setup for any length of time.

People have been keeping chickens and ducks since before recorded history began. All of the guesswork regarding what food they need in order to survive has been eliminated. There are many forms of commercial feed on the market for all types of fowl at all ages. There is, however, quite a bit of difference between the feed prepared for poultry raised for food and

FEEDING

those raised as pets. Your pet shop proprietor can advise you on the types of feed your pet will need to be healthy and hearty.

CHICKS AND CHICKENS

A paper or plastic picnic plate can be used as the first feeding dish for baby chicks in their brooders. Small wooden feed hoppers can also be used, but metal hoppers are most sanitary since germs cannot live on metal surfaces. Your pet shop owner will probably have ready-made chick feed hoppers in stock. If not, he'll be able to suggest suitable alternatives. If you have to change hoppers for some reason, always leave the one the chicks have become accustomed to in the brooder for a short time. This will help make the transition easier.

Choosing a chick feed is easy. Just select one of the commercial baby chick feeds and follow the directions provided by the manufacturer. Again, your pet shop proprietor will be able to suggest the kind you will need. Most experts suggest a high efficiency broiler chick feed or starter ration that is rich in vitamin D. Most of these are also medicated to help control coccidiosis, a bacterial infection to which chicks are highly susceptible.

Baby chicks are born hungry. They can be fed a starter ration as soon as they are placed in their brooders. You don't need separate hoppers for each chick. Several of them should be able to eat simultaneously. Make certain that ample food is available first thing in the morning. The hopper should be quite full, but the chicks should be allowed to clean up the food at least once a day.

Sometimes chicks won't eat. This may be because of trauma induced by being moved, or not having their mother near by, or having their hopper suddenly changed from something familiar. Whatever the reason, these chicks have to be shown how to eat or they will starve. If you find one chick who won't eat, sprinkle chick-size corn in a shallow pan and gently dip its beak into it. The commercial foods prepared for

White Wyandottes, commercially raised, are fed scientifically compounded feeds. You can buy this same feed from your local feed store.

chicks will give you a good guideline concerning the proper size to which the corn should be ground. Keep both mash and corn meal available to the picky chicks in separate containers for a couple of days. Afterwards, remove the corn pan and sprinkle a small amount of the corn on top of the regular food in the hopper. This method gently acquaints the chicks to their mash. They may have digestive problems, so it's also wise to sprinkle a small amount of insoluble grit, chick-size, over the mash.

At four to six weeks of age, chicks can have grains added to their diet. Allow the chicks to consume as much grain as they can over a 30-minute period; then remove their grain pan. Mash should always be made available to the chicks. Since both grains and mash are available commercially, it's easy to follow the manufacturer's directions regarding the proper proportions as your chicks grow and mature. By three weeks, they should have green foods in their diet too. Your pet shop owner is, once again, the best source of information as to the specific green foods baby chicks need. However, never include coarse, long-stemmed grasses in the baby chicks' diet.

As is true with all birds, baby chicks require plenty of water at all times. If you find a chick that won't drink, you'll have to treat it just as you did with the ones who refused to eat. Gently push its beak into the water until it gets the idea.

A water fountain can be easily made from ordinary items. Find an empty fruit can and clean it thoroughly with soap and water and rinse it completely. Then bore two tiny holes on opposite sides about three-quarters of an inch from the lip of the can. Fill the can with fresh water and place a clean aluminum pie plate on the top and turn it over. This handy waterer should then be carefully centered on a small wire mesh platform. This will prevent the chicks from stepping into damp litter. This fountain, and all hoppers and waterers, should be placed by the edge of your brooder except in cases where the chicks are, at first, reluctant to look for food and drink.

When your chicks have reached eight weeks of age, they should gradually be changed from the starter ration to a growing or developing ration. You may also want to add some salt to their diet on a regular basis. Developing young chickens also need some succulent green foods in their daily diet as well as some corn if it hasn't already been added. It's an excellent supplement to a chick's growing ration. You can change the chickens' diet to whatever commercially mixed foods you like until pullets have matured to laying age. Keep chickens on growing ration until that time and then gradually make the change-over.

Many chicken experts recognize three separate systems of chicken feeding: mash and grain, all mash, and all pellet. All of these are supplemented by a healthy portion of fresh greens.

If the all-mash system is used, it is wise to scatter some pellets into your chickens' litter so their scratching habits keep it stirred. If you use the mash and grain system, then scatter some of the grain in the litter for the same reason. Alfalfa leaf meal, corn gluten meal, cottonseed meal, milk by-products, peanut meal, soybean meal, and wheat bran all may be used as supplementary foods for mash diet.

Barley, grain sorghums, wheat, oats, and yellow corn are used as supplementary foods for the grain and mash diet.

Facing page: A very popular breed is the Polish, which is a dwarf, crested breed. There are other silky-haired breeds.

Although some pet owners are not prepared to care for laying hens, there are high-energy layer mashes available commercially for these birds. Diets for laying hens can be supplemented by bran and molasses which act as a tonic and mild laxative. Pellets can be added to their diet to give them some variety.

The old saying, "Rare as hens' teeth," is true. Chickens, like all other birds, have no teeth. They digest their food by swallowing insoluble grit which breaks up their food in their gizzards so they can digest it. Grit should be made available to the chickens at all times. Water as well should always be readily and easily obtainable.

All food and water hoppers should be cleaned daily. Leftover food, as long as it is still dry, can be mixed with the fresh. Be sure all hoppers are full in the morning.

DUCKLINGS AND DUCKS

As is the case with pet chickens, most of the groundwork regarding the feeding of ducklings and ducks is already taken care of. The centuries that have passed while humans have taken care of ducks has resulted in exceptional blends of duck food expertly balanced for good health and growth. Your pet shop owner will be fully familiar with everything you'll need from the very beginning. Commercial duck food is also very reasonable in price. A three-pound bag of duck mash will give your pet ducklings a healthy beginning. You'll also need a small bag of grit to aid the duck's digestion since, like all birds, ducks, geese, and swans require a certain amount of this kind of gravel to assist their gizzards in grinding any food they eat.

Duck mash is served dry to your ducklings. The ducks themselves will instinctively moisten it with water. Make certain you always provide an ample supply of fresh, clean water for your birds as they eat. In the wild, birds have to forage for all of their food. Even in a large barnyard, well-fed ducks enjoy foraging around for additional food and grit material to supplement their normal diet of mash. Since most pet ducks are more confined and cannot forage in a pond, they require you to provide a little fish or meat-meal in their mash diet. A good food supplement stocked by most good pet shops is regular coarse-grind tropical fish food. This is usually made of fresh meal and is ideal for the

Facing page: Children must be taught the proper way to handle their pets. Birds rarely enjoy being handled...squeezing is dangerous to their well being.

purpose. Since your pet is restricted in its foraging, you'll discover that it will need more grit than the ducklings who are able to wander over a field or garden terrain ingesting sand, little snails, etc.

Naturally, to maintain the health of your young ducklings, you must always remember to serve their food and water in clean containers. Flat glass trays are the best dish for ducks. It's easy to notice when they're dirty, they're easy to clean, and they're easy for the ducks to use. All stale or uneaten food should be removed. If any scraps are left, they may become moldy and cause serious health problems for any ducks unfortunate enough to eat them–they might even prove fatal.

Another alternative feeding dish is a ceramic flowerpot saucer. These are excellent duck feeding dishes because they allow the ducks to walk around them without stumbling. These saucers are also shallow, so the birds are easily able to shovel their food from the saucer's flat surface. Just as with the glass dishes, these types of saucers are easy to wash and clean.

Speaking of water depth, it is important that a baby duckling's first water trough not be too deep. If it is, there is a danger that the duckling could fall in and become chilled. On the other hand, the water dish cannot be too shallow either. Young ducklings must be able to dip their heads into their water. They do this to keep their eyes clean and to remove food particles from their heads and backs. If they can't clean the food off of themselves, the other ducks may peck at the leftovers and pull out the duckling's downy feathers at the same time.

To provide a continual source of grass for your ducks to eat, you need to build a wooden frame and cover it with wire mesh. Place it over an area where you have recently planted new grass. When the young grass seedlings sprout and grow through the wire mesh, the ducklings will be able to nip off the grass tops without pulling out the very smallest seedlings by the roots. They'll eat all they can; but new grass will continually grow and replenish their supply.

As your ducklings grow older, their dietary needs change as well. As they grow larger, you can add chicken scratch to their diet. The older they get, the more ducks like to forage on grass and weeds, insects and snails, meat and fish scraps. You can either capture and collect these on your own (which can be an excellent learning experience for children) or you can buy such things commercially at your neighborhood pet shop. If snail poisons and garden sprays have been used in the area, don't collect supplementary food items from there since these could be dangerous for the ducklings. Such pesticides should never be used in any area where your ducks will be feeding.

Avoid protein foods in excess. Too much protein will result in too many shell-less eggs being laid. Laying ducks eat great quantities of

Ducks are mainly vegetarians. Many berries are poisonous to ducks, so keep them away from wild berries of all kinds. If you can't eat them, neither should the ducks.

shelling materials. Such ducks should have a large container of limestone, grit, or oyster shell (or a mixture of these materials) easily available at all times. Use a familiar container for the shelling materials. Ducks like a strict routine and don't like changes during their rearing and maturing stages before they reach the laying age. For this same reason, you should not let different people feed them. They quickly get used to one person attending to their needs and grow nervous or suspicious around anyone else. Whoever takes care of them should remember to move slowly and quietly around the ducks so they become used to their presence.

With all pets, your best source of information regarding their health is your local veterinarian. If any health problems arise, the veterinarian is the first person you should contact. If you do not know of a local veterinarian, your pet shop owner or another pet owner could probably recommend a good one. Not only will the veterinarian be able to help your animal,

HEALTH

but he will be able to further instruct you regarding preventive measures to take in the future, ensuring a long, happy, and healthy life for your pet.

YOUR CHICKEN'S HEALTH

Chicken diseases are actually easiest to control through prevention. The chicken has been so commonly kept by humans for so long that its upkeep has developed into an almost exact science. There is little mystery left regarding the kinds of diseases which attack chickens and their cures. The most common "cure" given by chicken raising experts is prevention. And the best prevention is a safe environment for your birds, be they pets or otherwise.

Cleanliness is responsible for warding off countless health difficulties. Over the years, a specific and seasonal routine has been developed for keeping chicken houses as clean and germ-free as possible. (Remove all of your chickens before you begin this disinfecting procedure.) The cycle begins each and every fall, when your chicken house should be thoroughly disinfected. This is accomplished with one part of three to five percent creosol to 100 parts water solution or a two percent lye solution. The strong creosol solution can be used in a spray. This disinfectant is very potent; when using it, you should wear eye protection, rubber gloves and boots for your own safeguard.

You should then clean all the equipment that comes in contact with the chickens or their house with a disinfectant red mite paint. The chemical fumes from these solutions are poisonous and they linger for quite a while so, if at all possible, keep chickens out of the shelter for an entire month.

Even with these precautions, common diseases may still strike your chickens. Some of these include influenza, coccidiosis, and Newcastle. Certain symptoms should be watched for so you can catch these ailments in early stages. If you see any of the following, there should be cause for concern: bloody diarrhea; depression; emaciation; loss of appetite; nervousness; constantly ruffled feathers; shrill cries; cold symptoms; stiff or wobbly walk; or swollen parts. Veterinarians have certain vaccines or medications for some of the diseases that cause some of these symptoms, but the sad fact is that diseased chickens should be destroyed before they infect the entire flock. If you have only one pet chicken and you keep its surroundings clean, infection caused by contact with other birds should be minimal.

Chickens have no teeth. Birds in general have no teeth though some, like parrots, have beaks with which they can bite. To give your chicken a pill, simply pull his mouth open and drop the pill in, then gently shove it down his throat.

Another preventive measure involves eliminating dampness in your chicken house. Examine the vicinity just inside all the windows, doors, or other openings where litter may get wet from snow or rain. Always completely remove from the chicken house any wet or caked litter which may have accumulated there. The same should be done with any food materials that have been dampened by the weather or from water spillage.

Birds are messy creatures. They are forever scattering water around their drinking hoppers and making their litter damp. However, walking on the damp litter is not where the danger lies. What is hazardous for their health is eating grains that have fallen into this damp litter and become moldy. Eating moldy foods can lead to many health problems.

A properly constructed chicken shelter will have removable boards or pits beneath the roost to catch droppings and keep them away from your chickens. You can prevent dampness from collecting on these boards or in the pits by adding hydrated lime or superphosphate. This can also be added to the floor litter to reduce accumulated moisture.

You should check your chickens every day. If you find that you have a problem with maggots, apply a powder solution of aldrin, malathion, or dieldrin to the droppings pit or board. Bury all poultry offal.

If you've built your chicken house large enough, quietly enter it after dark. Walk around and check the edges and corners for drafts. Seal them up as soon as possible. If you have glass windows in your chicken house, make sure they are cleaned often. A chicken house needs lots of sunshine.

A gurgling sound from your chickens is a common cold symptom. Birds sitting on the floor instead of up on the roost may also be ill. If one bird does appear sickly, immediately remove it from the others so whatever it's suffering from will not spread. It's also a good suggestion to keep older chickens separated from the young birds.

Although it is advisable to quietly check your chickens at night, don't make a practice of allowing others to come in and inspect. As few people as possible should go in and out of your chicken shelter.

Flies are not only a nuisance but also transmit diseases such as cholera, fowl pox, tuberculosis, and tapeworm infestations. Residual sprays can be used against these pests, but observing basic sanitation helps to ward off most of them. Feed bags should be protected from flies, mice, and rats; this is best handled by buying feed only in new or disinfected bags.

There are several kinds of lice which affect chickens. You can prevent your pets from suffering from these parasites by painting the top of your roosts with a commercial nicotine sulfate preparation available from your pet shop, hardware store, or perhaps your local drug store. Three or four paintings, spaced two or three days apart, will create fumes

Facing page: If you've been a good parent and trained your children in how to raise their chick, what happens when it grows up? You can keep it as a pet or utilize it for your own table (hard to do) or give it to a farmer to add to his flock.

It is a good idea to periodically douse your chicken with parasite-killing medication recommended by your vet or local feed supplier.

which will rise up through your chickens' feathers and kill the lice. Of course these fumes are harmless to the chickens.

Another common parasite, the red mite, attaches itself to chickens during the night from nooks and crannies in chicken shelters. Red mites can be eliminated by painting your roost supports and your nest boxes with a commercial preparation for this purpose. Since these parasites are seasonal, this should be done in April. Repeat the procedure in mid-July or early August (in the northern hemisphere).

Finally, the yard area surrounding the chicken house should also be kept as clean and as free of trash as possible.

As is true with every kind of pet, your local veterinarian is always on hand with the most up-to-date knowledge about the well-being of your animals. He or she is the first one you should call whenever any questions about your pet's health come up.

Your local pet shop proprietor or a fellow chicken owner will be able to direct you to a reputable veterinarian, who will aid you in maintaining the current and future health of your pet.

YOUR DUCK'S HEALTH

Fortunately ducks are extremely hardy animals that are easy to raise. There are very few diseases or sicknesses easily acquired by them. As with most pets, the best way to deal with any ailment is to prevent it from happening in the first place. Prevention is your first line of defense.

Ducks can suffer from rheumatism if their bedding is allowed to become wet or soggy. It's true that they like water to swim in, but they don't like to be wet for extended times or when they're sleeping. They instinctively know when they want to be dry. Don't try to second-guess this instinct. Keep their bedding changed frequently and this problem will be avoided.

Speaking of water, remember to have drinking water available all the time. If small ducklings have been denied water for too long a time,

Newly born chicks, only one day old, are already able to take feed. Mixed in with the feed can be supplements of vitamins, minerals, or medications recommended by your veterinarian.

If your chicken is your pet, you can tell if he is ill. This bird is alert, clear eyed and healthy.

they tend to over-drink when they finally find water. This could lead to the "staggers" and even kill them. Thirsty baby ducklings can drink themselves to death. Ducks also have to be able to reach water for removing food from their bodies and eyes. Stale food can cause eye sores on ducks. If this does occur, you can obtain a small tube of mercuric oxide ophthalmic ointment at your local pet shop or at a drug store. The druggist or pet shop owner will be able to advise you regarding how much of this ointment to use to help cure the ducklings' sore eyes.

If serving dishes are not cleaned frequently or properly, stale food collects. If moldy food is eaten, diarrhea could result, as could a disease called aspergillosis, which can be fatal to the ducklings. Aspergillosis symptoms include labored breathing, gasping, increased thirst, loss of appetite, sleepiness, emaciation, and a dark coloring of the skin making it appear blue (cyanosis). You may also observe nervous disorders such as the ducklings twisting their necks. These are symptoms of aspergillosis as well. Consult your veterinarian for treatment suggestions. Dry bedding, a constant supply of clean water, and fresh food in clean dishes will help ensure strong, healthy ducks.

Although ducks are hardy animals, they are not immune to diseases and other health problems. After prevention, the best defense is close observation of symptoms. Reporting symptoms accurately to your veterinarian will help quickly and properly to correct the condition, if possible.

If you note something unusual about your ducks, either in appearance or in manner, write it down. If other symptoms crop up later, putting all of this information together could lead to a clearer understanding of the problem. Remember, if symptoms show up in one bird, remove it from the others to stop the spread of any infection.

Anatipestifer infection (or new duck disease) is blood poisoning that occurs in ducklings during the first eight weeks of their lives and is caused by bacteria. It also shows up in chickens and turkeys from time to time. It can affect your older ducks, too, but to a much lesser degree.

Anatipestifer infection appears suddenly with mild coughing and sneezing. Later symptoms include a discharge from the duck's nostrils and eyes, tremors of the head and neck, and greenish diarrhea. Finally, the birds lose their balance, drop into a coma, and expire. On some occasions, the duck will lie on its back and flap its webbed feet. The liver and spleen may start swelling up due to dehydration. Anatipestifer infection sometimes brings on pneumonia as well.

The recognized treatment for anatipestifer infection is a combination of penicillin and streptomycin, or sulfaquinoaline, the latter being

If a bird is ill, it usually will not eat. Thus the nicely round crops on these three ducklings indicates they are well fed and, therefore, probably healthy.

less toxic. Once you have removed the sick birds to separate brooders, you'll have to disinfect the brooders they were in. Don't put healthy birds back in them for at least two to four weeks.

Water belly (or ascites) affects ducks by an accumulation of fluids inside the abdominal cavity. Ingesting too much salt can cause this problem, as can certain malfunctions of the duck's organs. The symptoms to look for include the bird's standing more upright than normal and swelling of the abdomen. Treatment will not completely cure the condition and it's likely to recur. Unfortunately, the best and most humane way to treat ascites is by destroying the duck.

Limberneck (or western duck sickness) is actually botulism–in other words, food poisoning. The toxin in decayed ingested meat produced by *Clostridium botulinum* bacteria causes limberneck. Luckily, this disease is not spread from duck to duck, but only by ingesting the toxin. If the birds eat maggots which have been feeding on a rotting carcass, they can contract the disease. In the wilds of the western United States and in Canada, ducks die by the millions each year after eating the decaying vegetation prevalent in the areas.

The most common and recognizable symptom, which appears very shortly after ingesting the toxin, is paralysis of the duck's neck muscles, as well as, in some cases, the wings and neck. If the amount of toxin is large enough, the duck could die in 12 to 24 hours.

The condition has to be diagnosed rapidly if the duck is to have a chance for survival. The ducks should be removed from their pens immediately and the source of the toxin discovered. Wet, spoiled food is the most likely cause in the case of domesticated ducks. Don't let your ducks eat anything else for a full 24 hours. Feed them about one-sixth of an ounce of epsom salts mixed with a tiny amount of clean water or wet mash. Mixing about one-quarter cup of a stock solution of potassium permanganate into two gallons of drinking water may be enough to flush out the toxin from the animal's system. Your veterinarian can inject your bird with two to four cc of *C. botulinum* antitoxin. The condition should improve over the next 12 hours; but if there's little or no change, a repeat injection will probably be needed.

Duck plague (or duck virus enteritis) is a contagious disease caused by a herpes virus. It also affects geese and swans. This disease is spread by contaminated duck droppings in the birds' feed or bathing water. It enters the body through the nostrils, the mouth, the cloaca, or through skin cuts. One of the symptoms is extreme thirst. You might also see bloody diarrhea, listlessness, loss of appetite, droopy wings, soiled vents, swollen eyelids, or nasal discharge. Ducklings who suffer from this virus will become dehydrated, lose weight, show blood on their vents, and have bluish colored beaks. Muscovies are more likely to die from this disease than other breeds of duck. There is no cure. Prevention by sanitation is the best defense in this case.

One disease that is fatal to ducklings under four weeks of age is the highly contagious duck virus hepatitis (or baby duck disease). There have been reports of minor outbreaks in other breeds, but it is most fatal to the Pekins. An affected duck will be found lying on its side, drawing its head back towards its tail while paddling its feet. Within a week, the duckling will die. Check with your veterinarian regarding injections of antiserum into the muscle of the infected duckling.

Almost all domesticated varieties of duck originated with the Mallards. They have developed into smaller and larger sizes and many colors. The more obscure the color, the better it might be as a pet because it is still further removed from the wild Mallard strains. For a pet though, all you should be concerned about is how large it will be when fully grown...and does it fly!

Many people who prefer conventional pets such as dogs and cats have difficulty understanding why anyone would want a pet such as a chicken or duck. They believe that you can't take them for walks and you can't play with them. Those who have successfully raised chicks and ducks as pets know that this is far from the truth. Not only can you play with them, but they can learn tricks, they can learn to come to their owner when called, and they can show love and affection. All it takes is some time and patience.

YOUR PET

CHICKS AS PETS

Even though the majority of baby chicks are purchased for young children, the little yellow birds should not be handled by these small kids. If the child is used to a kitten or a puppy, he will naturally believe that a chick is just as sturdy as the more traditional pets. The majority of deaths to Easter pets is due to complications arising from serious injury by careless treatment.

Of course, picking up the chick and feeling its soft feathers and rapid little heartbeat is exactly what children will want to do. After all, what good is a pet if you can't play with it? Are those dog and cat owners right after all? Is sitting and watching all you can safely do with a pet chicken? Thankfully, the answer to all of these questions is "No." All your child will need is some preliminary instruction and he will be able to safely handle the pet chicken as long as he's careful and as long as it's not done too often. Actually, handling of the chicken will get it used to its owner in an intimate and friendly way.

If your child (or children) *has* to pick up the chick, instruct him to carefully place the palms of both hands on each side of the chick's body with the fingers well beneath and to lift the little thing very gently. Remind him never to press or grasp the breast of the chick.

Those dog and cat owners who have not been witness to a well-trained pet chicken are often amazed at how tame, responsive, and friendly it is. They'll be astounded at how it rides on its owner's shoulder and how it can even accept being led on a light leash, pulled around in a wagon, or ride proudly perched on a bicycle handlebar. The fact is, anyone, child or adult, can easily teach a pet chicken a couple of tricks. He must remember to wait, however, until the bird has become accustomed to his voice and has been assured that his hands are gentle.

If you received your pet chicken as a baby chick, it's best to wait until it has become fully feathered before trying to train it in any manner. Older chickens are easier to train than young chicks.

Observe your chicken closely and take note of the actions and mannerisms it performs daily. Based on these everyday actions, devise a

Chicks can be taught lots of tricks if you have the patience, but keep in mind that they cannot be housebroken.

trick that the chicken will have no difficulty in performing. For example, since chickens naturally enjoy pecking and scratching and flying short distances up to a perch, one or more of these natural abilities can be correlated with a particular simple noise such as the ringing of a bell or the rattling of tin cans. The chicken can be taught to make the noise (ring the bell or rattle the can) as long as there is positive reinforcement (i.e., the incentive of food). In order to perform a trick, the chicken has to associate the action of the trick with obtaining food. Once this is established, the chicken will perform the trick every time it wants to eat.

One of the simplest tricks to teach a chicken to do is to ring its own dinner bell. Before starting the first bell-ringing lesson, don't feed your pet chicken for 24 hours. (Water, however, must be available as always.) Next, attach a bell to a cord and suspend it within reach of the bird's beak. Pet shops have bells designed for parakeet cages which are ideal for this purpose. Prepare a tin cup or plate with food and show it to the pet as you ring the bell. Immediately allow the chicken to eat a few grains of the food. Don't hesitate for even a moment before offering the grain. As soon as the chicken has had the opportunity to taste the food, remove it. Ring the bell once more and quickly offer the food again. Repeat the whole procedure a number of times, but be careful not to wear your chicken out.

The second bell-ringing lesson should follow 12 hours after the first. During that time, don't feed your chicken at all. However, continually pet and love it during these 12-hour fasts. After several days of this routine, discontinue rewarding the chicken for merely hearing the bell. Change the routine so you feed it only if it approaches the bell. After it gets used to this routine, let it eat only if it actually pecks at the bell.

When the time comes that the chicken is regularly pecking at the bell (which should be completely removed when the bell-ringing lessons are not in progress), place the cup a little distance from the bell and fill it with just a small amount of the grain. Soon you'll see the chicken begin to whirl around after it has rung the bell and run to the cup to eat.

When all the food is eaten, the chicken will, of its own accord, return to ring the bell expecting to obtain more treats. Make sure you reward it each time or the training will soon be forgotten. This is the most humane method known for training just about any animal. The scientific term for this behavior is *conditioned reflex*. It was discovered by the famous Russian physiologist Ivan Petrovich Pavlov in experiments with his dogs. You can make the trick more complex later on by teaching the pet to jump through a hoop before reaching the cup of food. The conditioned reflex will remain with the chicken indefinitely.

Your pet chicken will come to depend on you for food just as you depend on it to perform its tricks and remain loyal and friendly. Always remember to take care of its daily needs. If you have to leave, remember that a weekend is about as long a period to safely leave your birds on their own. If you do leave, be sure to leave plenty of drinking water and mash or grain in easy reach. Don't leave foods that can spoil if left uneaten, such as fresh greens or fruit. If you have to go away for a longer time than 48 hours, teach a neighbor how to care for your pet–and leave a copy of this book around for handy reference.

While pet owners don't immediately think about it, they must remember that their female chickens will be laying eggs someday. Most

Is there anything better for your child than to get an Easter egg and an incubator? Then he takes care of the resulting hatchlings until they lay their own eggs and he gives the eggs and incubator to other friends, etc.

of the time, chicks are sold without regard to sex. You don't know if you're getting a hen or a rooster unless the chicks have been separated by a professional. Sexed chicks usually cost more than random ones since sexing them by a professional costs money. If you do end up with a hen, you may want to try your hand at hatching some eggs yourself.

In fact, you may want to raise a chick from hatching; this can be done without a rooster. All you have to do is obtain an unwashed but suitably sanitized egg from a poultry dealer. If you have a willing hen, you can hatch it under her or you can rent some incubator space from the aforementioned poultry dealer.

If you get your own incubator, remember that it will have to be placed in an area free from drafts, where it won't be jostled by passers-by. Modern incubators are electrically powered, but you should be aware of the danger of possible power outages.

Before placing eggs in an incubator, you should have it in operation for a few days. Place the eggs inside with the small end down. They will require three full weeks to hatch under a uniform temperature of 102°F (39°C) for the first two days and 103°F (39.5°C) from then on.

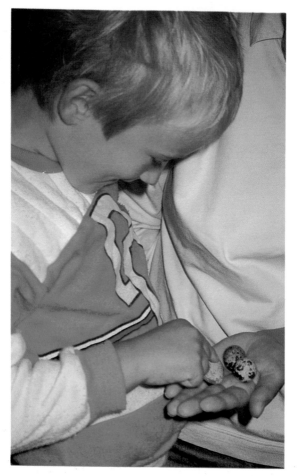

It is possible but not advisable for you to collect the eggs of wild birds and hatch them in your incubator. They probably will hatch but will you have the expertise to handfeed the chicks?

Fancy strains of chickens and ducks can often be bought as fertilized eggs which you hatch yourself.

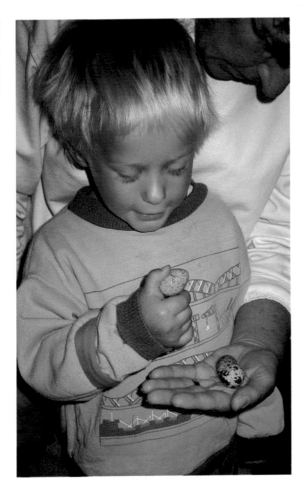

On the third day, you should begin to turn the eggs twice a day until two days prior to hatching. The best way to remember this is to mark the eggs. Do this quickly so the eggs do not get cold. You can check the fertility of the eggs by holding them up to the light and checking for dark outlines.

As soon as they hatch, the chicks will be observed moving toward the light at the front of the incubator when they drop to the lower compartment. Take them out, cover them warmly and transport them to their brooder.

DUCKS AS PETS

Ducks are extremely imitative birds. A duck will become attracted to and dependent upon a child who's taking care of it more quickly than any other fowl. If you raise your duck in the company of chickens, you'll soon discover that the duckling will begin to think of itself as a chicken! It will adopt the mannerisms and habits of the surrounding chickens rather than maintain its duckling heritage.

If a young duckling is raised by a child without other pets, the bird becomes solely attached to that child, playing with the child's toys and following the youngster wherever it goes. This is why many psychologists feel that the duckling makes a perfect companion for any child from six years on up.

While ducklings get used to children very quickly and completely, it is only a fully-feathered duck that can be trained to do tricks quickly. However, before any duck can be taught to perform, it must be tamed, and taming may take more time than training.

To tame a duck a youngster must remember not to excite the animal. A duck can be quickly calmed if its owner does not make any swift, sudden, or startling movements in the duck's presence. Talk quietly in a low voice to reassure the bird while you softly stroke its feathers. Before you can attempt to teach a duck to do tricks, you must be able not only to pet the duck, but also be able to call it to you and pick it up.

Naturally, ducks have physical limitations which make some tricks impossible to do no matter how much training they receive. It is always important to select a trick that the duck *can* do. Don't try to train it to do pulling tricks with its bill like chickens are often taught. The chicken's beak is much more suited to this kind of stunt than the duck's flat bill. It would be better to devise a stunt that takes advantage of the shoveling action of the duck's bill or its expert swimming skill.

One trick that is often seen involves ducks sliding down a short trough into water. The ducks enjoy it and can execute it easily without harm. Once learned, the ducks can perform this trick automatically. The set-up rewards the ducks' sliding action with food grain falling into a pan. When the duck slides down the trough, the food is released. The ducks have learned to recognize the sound of the grain falling into the pan and

Facing page: There is probably no better gift (from the child's point of view) than a pair of chicks or ducks. But be sure to give a book about their care along with the birds.

to perform the slide to get more food.

One large pet shop reported attracting quite a bit of attention with a sliding duck act such as this. A number of ducks were taught to do the trick and, when one tired, it was replaced.

One delightful trick a youngster can train his pet duck to do is to turn the pages of a large book. All one needs to prepare for this is a bell, a pan of feed, a bookstand or rack to hold the book open, a book and, of course, a duck.

Once the duck is completely tame, refrain from feeding it for a full 24 hours. Do not deny water during this time, but don't allow it to have any other food. The duck should be shown some extra love and attention during this time, with gentle petting and taming exercises, so it won't feel abandoned.

Prepare a pan of food. Set the book up on the stand and hold the bell in one hand. (Have all of this ready before setting the duck up by the book.) Always remaining in the same spot, show the feed in the pan and allow the duck to shovel some food while ringing the bell. Remove the food. Now, ring the bell again and give the food again.

Once again, this is the most humane method known for training just about any animal. There is never any punishment with this method; instead the duck is always rewarded when he does the right thing. After a remarkably short time, the duck's response is conditioned by the ringing and it will come to expect food every time it hears the ringing bell.

Once this conditioning is accomplished, you'll see the duck looking for food the second the bell sounds. Don't delay producing the food pan as soon as the bell is rung. A delay of as little as two seconds can reduce as much as 50% of the value of the reward in the fowl family. Always be ready with all props and rewards every second during these training sessions.

After several days of training, you can advance with the second segment of the trick. Don't let the duck go a full 24 hours without eating before the next session. Twelve hours of fasting is sufficient. Place a large book on the frame and open it, turning the pages back at the corners. Leave the duck alone until it approaches the book, then ring the bell and offer it the food. As the duck gets closer and closer to the book's pages, ring the bell and reward it with more food. Stop rewarding the duck for merely getting close to the entire book. If your duck gets too full of feed, stop.

During later sessions, wait to ring the bell until the duck actually

Facing page: Take a close look. Does this duckling look ugly to you? Their down is like fine silk.

puts its bill on a page; then when it actually puts a page in its mouth; and finally, when it pulls on the page. Eventually, the duck will be able to be taught to pull and walk with each page, turning them for food.

One of the most amazing things about a duck is that, once trained to do a trick, it can be left out in a barnyard for as long as two years or more without performing and it will still be able to do the trick again as soon as it sees the same props. This has nothing to do with intelligence or memory; it is only a natural result of training a pet that happens to have a very strong hunger drive.

Since your pet duck will come to depend on you for everything, don't forget to take care of it every day. A weekend is about as long a time to safely leave your birds alone. If you do leave, be sure to leave plenty of drinking water and food available. Don't leave foods such as fresh greens or fruit since if they go uneaten for too long, they can spoil.

If you have to leave for longer than 48 hours, instruct a neighbor how to care for your pet duck, and, as with chickens, leave a copy of this book around for handy reference.

A group of duck families goes for a communal swim. The ducklings always stay close to the parents. If you raise them, they will follow you like a puppy.

Ducklings get along with chicks, but they usually ignore each other.

INDEX

alfalfa, 36
Anatidae, 13
anatipestifer, 49
Araucana, 10
Ascites, 50
aspergillosis, 48
Aylesbury, 14
bantam, 11
Brahma, 8, 11
brooder, 20
Buff 14
cat, 20
Cayuga, 14
chick feed, 34
Chinese, 8
Clostridium, 50
coccidiosis, 43
Cochin, 11
comb, 8
conditioned reflex, 54
cottonseed meal, 36
crop, 8
diarrhea, 43
dog, 20
drakes, 13
duck virus hepatitis, 51
feeding, 34
flat bills, 13
food hopper, 26
French Houdan, 8
Fuligulinae, 14
Gallus domesticus, 6
Gallus gallus, 6
geese, 13
gizzard, 8
Greek, 8
grit, 38
health, 42
hen's teeth, 38
housing, 20
humane society, 4
humidity, 23

incubator, 55
influenza, 43
Italian Rooster, 7
La Fleche, 8
Lanshan, 11
Leghorns, 9
lice, 44
limberneck, 50
limestone, 41
litter, 36
Malay fowl, 8
Mars, 8
Merginae, 13
mites, 46
Muscovy, 14
natural diets, 6
New Hampshires, 9, 10
Newcastle disease, 42
oyster shell, 41
Pekin duck, 14
pets, 52
pheasant, 6
Plymouth, 9
plywood, 32
ponds, 29
quail, 6
Red Jungle Fowls, 12
rheumatism, 46
Rhode Island reds, 9
roosts, 27
Rouen, 14
sea ducks, 14
starter ration, 34
swans, 13
sweat glands, 19
training, 53
transporting, 17
trauma, 34
tricks, 53
turkey, 6
ventilation, 19